THE SOMME

Sarah Ridley

W
FRANKLIN WATTS
LONDON • SYDNEY

Franklin Watts
First published in Great Britain in 2016 by
The Watts Publishing Group

Editor: Julia Bird
Designer: sprout.uk.com
Picture researcher: Diana Morris

Picture credits:
2nd Lt T K Aitken/IWM: 43. Australian Official Photographer/IWM: 42.
By Kind Permission of the descendants of Maurice Baker: 12b, 32. Lt J
W Brooke/IWM: 12t, 19b, 27, 30b, 34, 35. Lt Ernest Brooks/IWM: front
cover b/g, 1 b/g, 3 b/g, 13b, 20, 22, 23, 25, 29, 37. Canadian War Museum/
CC Wikimedia: 18. Central London Recruiting Depot/IWM: 7c. Everett
Historical/Shutterstock: 9b. German Official Photographer/IWM: 4.
Brian Harris for CWGC/Alamy: 45tl. ILN/MEPL: 33, 38. Imperial War
Museum: 8, 10, 14, 15, 16, 17, 19t, 26, 31, 36, 39t, 39b, 41, 44. Ingalina/
Dreamstime: 45tr. Geoffrey Malins/IWM: front cover main, 1 main, 21.
Horace Nicholls/IWM: 6. Parliamentary Recruiting Committee/IWM:
5. Royal Engineers/IWM: 24. By Kind Permission of the descendants of
Robert Semple: 11. Sports & General PA/IWM: 7t. CC Wikimedia: 28, 30

Acknowledgements
The author and publishers would like to thank the following people
or organisations whose material is included in this book. The Baker
family acting on behalf of Rifleman Maurice Baker p 12, 27, 32 and 37.
Extracts from Malcolm Brown's *The Imperial War Museum Book of the
Somme*: Captain George McGowan p 15; Lieutenant Alfred Bundy p 22.
The Imperial War Museum Sound Archive/Voices of the First World War:
Private Donald Murray p 14; Private Walter Spencer p 16; Cecil Lewis,
fighter pilot with the Royal Flying Corps p 18; Stefan Westmann, Medical
Officer, German army p 19 and 21; Corporal Arnold Dale p 23; Marjorie
Llewellyn p 32; Private Leonard Davies p 35; Sergeant Charles Quinnell
p 36. The Wigglesworth family acting on behalf of Second Lieutenant/
Captain Robert Semple p 11.

Many thanks also to the following for permission to reproduce literary
material: the estate of George and Felix Powell for the chorus from 'Pack
up your troubles in your old kit bag' p 7; The Robert Graves Copyright
Trust for 'A Dead Boche' by Robert Graves p 29; Penguin Books for
the extract from Storm of Steel by Ernst Jünger, translated by Michael
Hofmann p 31; EMI Music Publishing for the chorus from 'Take me back
to dear old Blighty!' by Fred Godfrey, A J Mills and Bennett Scott p 36;
Barbara Levy as agent for George Sassoon for extract from his diary p 22
and 'They' by Siegfried Sassoon p 41.

ISBN 978 1 4451 4690 4

Printed in China

Franklin Watts
An imprint of
Hachette Children's Group
Part of The Watts Publishing Group
Carmelite House
50 Victoria Embankment
London EC4Y 0DZ

An Hachette UK Company
www.hachette.co.uk

www.franklinwatts.co.uk

FSC
MIX
Paper from
responsible sources
FSC® C104740
www.fsc.org

The soldier poets and writers featured in this book:

Laurence Binyon (1869–1943) Museum curator and poet, Laurence
Binyon, wrote his famous poem 'To the Fallen' at the very beginning
of the war. Too old for active service, in 1915 he volunteered with
the French Red Cross, working as an ambulance driver and medical
orderly.

Rupert Brooke (1887–1915) Already a published poet, Rupert Brooke
joined the navy at the outbreak of war. He died of blood poisoning,
probably as a result of a mosquito bite, on the way to Gallipoli.

Robert Graves (1895–1985) In 1914, Robert Graves had just left
school. He immediately volunteered, becoming an officer in the Royal
Welch Fusiliers. He almost died during the Battle of the Somme. After
the war, Graves became a full-time writer.

Ernst Jünger (1895–1998) German writer Ernst Jünger ran away
from school to join the German army. He fought throughout the war,
including the Battle of the Somme, and wrote several books about his
wartime experiences, including *Storm of Steel*, published in 1920.

Ewart Alan Mackintosh (1893–1917) University student, Ewart
Alan Mackintosh, joined the Seaforth Highlanders in 1914, won the
Military Cross, was wounded during the Battle of the Somme,
recovered in England then returned to active service. He was killed in
an attack on 21 November 1917.

Wilfred Owen (1893–1918) In 1915 Wilfred Owen enlisted and left
for the Western Front in January 1917. He suffered from shell shock,
came home to recover but returned to France in August 1918. He was
killed in action on 4 November 1918 – one week before the war ended.

Isaac Rosenberg (1890–1918) Artist and writer Isaac Rosenberg
was brought up in poverty and enlisted in 1915 as a way to provide an
income for his mother. He was killed in action on 1 April 1918.

Siegfried Sassoon (1886–1967) Siegfried Sassoon enlisted at the
outbreak of war and became an officer in the Royal Welch Fusiliers.
He was awarded the Military Cross for bravery in 1916, became
increasingly disillusioned by the war in 1917, but returned to active
service in 1918.

Contents

War breaks out

In the summer of 1914, war broke out in Europe. On 28 June Archduke Franz Ferdinand, heir to the Austro-Hungarian Empire, was assassinated by a Bosnian Serb. Over the next 37 days, his death, existing alliances between countries and decisions made by European politicians led to the outbreak of war.

German soldiers march through a square in Brussels, the capital of Belgium, in August 1914. When the Germans invaded Belgium, they violated a treaty signed by European powers, including Britain, which had guaranteed Belgium's neutrality.

War declared!

On 4 August 1914, following the German army's invasion of neutral Belgium, Britain and its empire declared war on Germany, which was already at war with France and Russia. Eventually, more than 30 nations became involved, either on the side of Britain, France and Russia (the Allies) or on the side of Germany and Austria-Hungary (the Central Powers). The conflict quickly became a world war, fought in locations across the world, including Africa and the Middle East.

The British Expeditionary Force

In August 1914 Britain's small professional army, the British Expeditionary Force (BEF), crossed the English Channel to support the French army in their fight against the German army in Belgium. Several battles were fought, but neither side could force a victory.

Trench warfare

The use of field guns firing enormous numbers of artillery shells one after the other made open warfare very difficult. By mid-November, this led the opposing armies to dig defensive trenches, stretching from the Swiss mountains to the Belgian coast, to protect their soldiers from incoming shells. For most of the war, soldiers fighting on this Western Front would try to break through the trench defences of their enemy and capture ground.

Volunteers

After war had been declared, thousands of British men queued at recruiting offices to enlist for the duration of the war. Within eight weeks, three-quarters of a million men had enlisted and the volunteers kept coming. They had all been following a different life path before August 1914, as schoolboys and university students, as employees of factories or shops, as teachers, trainees in banks and offices, errand boys or farm labourers.

Among the volunteers were several talented writers and artists, including Rupert Brooke, who joined the Royal Navy shortly after war was declared. The first verse of his poem, 'The Soldier' (top right), captures the idealistic spirit of the time.

The British government used posters to encourage men to join up and to spread other messages about the war. This 1915 poster shows civilians gradually transforming into soldiers.

The Soldier

If I should die, think only this of me:
That there's some corner of a foreign field
That is for ever England. There shall be
In that rich earth a richer dust concealed;
A dust whom England bore, shaped, made aware,
Gave, once, her flowers to love, her ways to roam,
A body of England's, breathing English air,
Washed by the rivers, blest by suns of home.

The 'Big Push'

At first, the British people had hoped the war would be over by Christmas. However, fighting continued throughout 1915, when efforts were made by each side to break the deadlock of trench warfare. In late 1915 and early 1916 a new plan, the 'Big Push', was developed. Now known as the Battle of the Somme, it would be one of the bloodiest battles ever fought.

STEP INTO YOUR PLACE

An army of volunteers

The British soldiers that arrived in the area of the River Somme in the spring of 1916 were mostly inexperienced volunteers, not professional soldiers.

Signing up and training

If the volunteer passed the brief medical examination, and was the correct age and nationality, he swore an oath of allegiance to the King and received 'the King's shilling'. Most volunteers became infantrymen in new battalions attached to existing regiments. Within days they found themselves in one of the many training camps that had sprung up across Britain. Here they learnt to follow orders and fight with a rifle and a bayonet. Endless drill exercises and route marches built up strength and stamina, while specific training was given on how to dig trenches and give first aid.

'Pals' battalions

Many men joined up alongside friends or work colleagues to form so-called 'Pals' or 'Chums' battalions. One of the first Pals battalions was the 10th Stockbrokers' Battalion, which formed in London in early August 1914, growing to 1,000 volunteers over the course of a few days. By the end of September, 50 towns, many of them in the north of England, had each raised at least one Pals battalion. The army also recruited junior officers into Pals battalions, such as the 18th Service Battalion of the University and Public Schools. What the army had quickly discovered was that if you allowed men to stay with their friends, many more would enlist.

New volunteers held a Bible as they promised to 'faithfully defend His Majesty, His Heirs and successors... against all enemies', and to obey all officers who were of higher rank than themselves.

Rifle training for the 'Grimsby Chums', September 1914, a Pals battalion which eventually became part of the Lincolnshire Regiment. The army was so overwhelmed by recruits in the autumn of 1914 that men had to wear their own clothes at first.

Rally to the flag

When Britain declared war on Germany, it automatically brought the countries of its empire into the war. Those already in the Indian army found themselves caught up in the conflict. In Canada, Australia and New Zealand young men rushed to join the armed forces. Many felt a strong loyalty to the 'mother country' since many of their parents or grandparents had been brought up there. Hundreds of thousands of men from across the British Empire saw active service in the war.

By late 1915 and early 1916, some of the volunteer soldiers started arriving in France. As they marched along the roads of northern France, they sang jaunty marching songs such as 'Pack up your troubles'. Here is the chorus:

Recruitment posters played a big part in encouraging men to enlist both in Britain and across the Empire.

'Pack Up Your Troubles in Your Old Kit Bag'

Pack up your troubles in your old kit bag
And smile, smile, smile
While you've a Lucifer* to light your fag,
Smile, boys, that's the style.

What's the use of worrying?
It never was worth while, so
Pack up your troubles in your old kit bag,
And smile, smile, smile.

(* Lucifer was a brand of matches)

Planning the 'Big Push'

In late December 1915, General Joffre, the French commander-in-chief, proposed a joint British-French attack along the section of the front line where the French and British armies met, near the River Somme. This was to be another attempt to break the deadlock of trench warfare.

The Battle of Verdun

French and British generals met again on 14 February 1916 and decided that the French and British armies would launch the attack in August 1916. However, on 21 February the German army launched its own attack on the fortified town of Verdun in north-east France. This battle continued for most of 1916, with enormous loss of life on both sides. With the French army focusing on the defence of Verdun, most of the responsibility for the 'Big Push' would have to lie with the British army.

a force of this size but, nevertheless, he set about planning and preparing for the 'Big Push' with meticulous care. Since the majority of the troops were volunteers, he assumed that they would not be able to follow a complicated battle plan. Instead of planning for the more usual army attack technique where one group of soldiers protected the advance of the other using rifle fire, he decided that wave after wave of soldiers would walk across the unoccupied area between the Allied and German armies, known as No Man's Land.

General Haig

General Sir Douglas Haig had been appointed commander-in-chief of the British army in France and Belgium in December 1915 – an army that had expanded massively since the outbreak of war. Haig had no experience of commanding

General Sir Douglas Haig, commander-in-chief of the British Army in France and Belgium.

This map shows the location of the front line in the area of the River Somme before 1 July 1916. The British planned to attack along a 24-km stretch of the front line and the French along a 13-km section to the south of them.

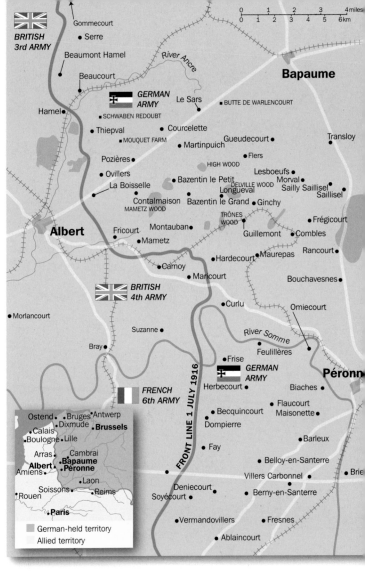

The artillery

Haig planned that troops would be able to walk across No Man's Land because a week-long bombardment of the German front line would have destroyed their machine gun posts and artillery. In addition, eight enormous mines would explode under the German trenches just before the attack commenced. A 'creeping barrage' of British artillery shells would provide a curtain of falling shells in front of the advancing British troops as they walked across No Man's Land.

With the German defences flattened by the bombardment, the men of the British Third Army would attack to the north, near Gommecourt, to divert German attention from the centre of the attack and inflict as much damage as possible. The British Fourth Army would break through in the centre, along a stretch of front line between Maricourt in the south and Serre in the north, to be followed through by the Reserve Army. To the south of the British line of attack, the French Sixth Army would launch their own attack.

In 1916, British munitions factories stepped up their output of guns, shells and other weapons that would be needed for the battle.

Life in the trenches

Battalion by battalion, British troops arrived in the area of the River Somme during late 1915 and the spring of 1916. The recruits had to quickly become accustomed to army life.

'Stand to'

Dawn and dusk were the most likely times for the Germans to attack so, just before dawn, all those in the front line trench stood ready with their rifles during the 'stand to' which was short for 'stand to arms'. Sentries scanned No Man's Land for any movement. About an hour later, if it was clear that no attack was coming, the order was given to 'stand down' and men started preparing breakfast. Then everyone went about their daily tasks until dusk, when the 'stand to arms' was repeated, followed by the evening meal.

Sentry duty

Soldiers took it in turns to act as the sentry on their section of the front line, keeping watch for any sign of an attack. Some of the soldiers with the best shooting skills became snipers, scanning the German front line trenches for the chance to shoot and kill. In turn, German snipers scanned the British front line trenches for an opportunity to kill British soldiers.

Official war artist, John Nash, painted *Stand to before Dawn* in 1918. He captures the grey light of dawn with soldiers peering over the parapet.

Mud, cold and danger

Everyday life could be brutal, particularly if the weather was cold or wet. Men endured cold weather by wrapping themselves up in their army greatcoats or huddling close to stoves or braziers. Since the trenches were effectively deep ditches, rain turned the soil to mud. A large number of soldiers developed 'trench foot', a skin condition caused by wearing damp socks. If left untreated, it could lead to infection or even amputation.

Danger was ever present. Second Lieutenant Robert Semple, writing to his younger sisters in October 1915, described the sudden death of a soldier in the front line, due to a sniper:

There are a lot of snipers round here. The other day… I saw a soldier who was outside the trench get hit in the back. He sat down backwards and for a minute went on smoking his pipe as if nothing had happened. Suddenly he seemed to feel the pain. He dropped his pipe and let out a yell. Immediately three or four men jumped up to pull him to safety. Amongst them was a Sergeant Major. The minute the Sergeant Major got out of the trench he was shot through the heart. A piece of very bad luck.

Second Lieutenant Robert Semple (see also above) drew this sketch of himself looking miserable in the French mud in a letter to his sisters written in November 1915.

Friendship

Soldiers had to share their waking and sleeping moments with the other men in their platoon, which consisted of about 50 men divided into four sections. As a result, they formed close bonds of friendship. In the Pals battalions (see pages 6–7), groups of soldiers already knew each other as they had worked in the same factories, played in the same football or cricket teams, been to the same schools or lived on the same streets.

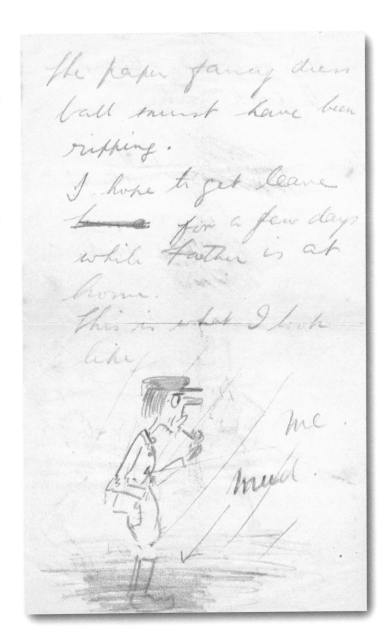

A soldier checks Mills bombs (hand grenades) outside a dugout in a trench near the River Somme, 1916. Dugouts helped protect men from bad weather and from exploding artillery shells.

Letters and parcels

Receiving letters or parcels from home brightened up a soldier's day. Rifleman Maurice Baker wrote many letters to his mother filled with requests for food or other items that would improve his quality of life. In one letter written in November 1915 he reassured his mother that the army had given him good gloves and a waterproof cape and listed the most important items he wanted her to send out:

Cigarettes. Matches. Candles. Café au lait. Cake. Potted meat. Chocolate. Never send jam. The army serve out a box of matches, about 20 cigarettes and tobacco. The cigs are made specially for soldiers and the quality is not wonderfully good. We may get more cigs when we are in the firing line. You can also send out some compact novels or the Story Teller *magazine.*

Rifleman Maurice Baker sent this photo of himself with a letter home in March 1916 when he was at a rest camp (see page 13), set back from the front line trenches.

Boredom and routine

After the morning 'stand down', men carried out their daily tasks. They spent some time repairing and improving the trenches, using sandbags filled with soil where the trench wall had collapsed or been damaged by a shell. They cleaned their rifles – and someone had to clean out the latrines, another name for a toilet.

Once the soldiers had completed their daily tasks, boredom could easily set in. Daytime was spent catching up on sleep, trying to keep themselves clean using a tiny amount of water, picking lice out of the seams of their clothing, reading, playing cards, smoking cigarettes and writing letters.

Army rations

The official army ration was adequate, but soldiers often went hungry as the army had run short of food supplies or was struggling to transport food up to front line troops. During the day, men ate tinned food or hard biscuits, which had to be soaked in tea or cups of hot water. In the evening, they waited for a hot meal – often beef stew – to be brought to them.

Danger

Even in the quiet sections of the front line, soldiers had to live with the constant threat of snipers, an attack or an exploding shell. If the shell was actually a canister of poison gas, and they didn't pull their gas masks on quickly enough, the gas reached their lungs, causing terrible damage or death.

In and out of the trenches

However, each company of soldiers was only in the front line, support or reserve trenches for a few days before being relieved by another company. Soldiers living in these three parallel rows of trenches were most at risk of being shelled or attacked, and they took part in any planned attacks. However, on average, soldiers spent about half their time out of the trenches altogether, in rest camps or billets set back from the front line trenches where men relaxed, received training and cleaned themselves and their uniforms.

Hot food was prepared in field kitchens, set back from the front line. Soldiers who were living near a field kitchen queued up for their dinner while those in front line trenches had to wait for it to be carried to them in big metal containers.

Preparations

All through late 1915 and early 1916 British soldiers, who had taken over much of this section of the front line from the French army, set about improving the defences of the front line trenches by digging and adding to the wire defences.

German defences

High in the skies above them, airmen of the Royal Flying Corps spied on the German front line and reported that they had well established front line defences. The Germans had occupied this area since the autumn of 1914. They had had plenty of time to dig deep underground shelters and fortified trenches, choosing the high ground as their line of defence.

Barbed wire

One of the ways to improve the front line was to repair and add to the barbed wire defences set up forward of the front line, in No Man's Land. Wiring parties, groups of soldiers who had been given this task, worked at night from February onwards, often within earshot of the German soldiers in their front line trenches.

Battle training

Private Donald Murray later recalled: 'In May they took us from the line, back about 10 km – right away from the fighting. And there they'd got the whole country flagged out, an exact replica of the German lines with little flags.

A wiring party at work at night in No Man's Land. Men set up wood or steel corkscrew pickets in the ground and stretched lengths of barbed wire between them.

We started practising the attack, ready for the big attack, this big attack that was to come.'

Men were also trained in how to throw hand grenades, lectured on gas warfare, drilled in hand-to-hand fighting with bayonets and marched around the French lanes to improve overall fitness.

Troops practise an attack at an army training school in France in August 1916.

Hard at work

The Germans, occupying the higher ground on the other side of No Man's Land, witnessed the build-up of equipment and supplies. For weeks, all the roads leading up to the front line were jammed with transport, as described by Captain George McGowan in a letter to his parents written in June 1916:

The roads leading to the front line were packed from early morning to early morning with transport stretching for miles back, bringing ammunition and stores. Working parties were hard at it day and night trench digging, cable burying, laying water pipes, digging gun pits and dugouts and carrying out scores of other fatigues necessary to ensure success.

Daily deaths

All through the months leading up to the 'Big Push', deaths and injuries occurred on a daily basis, as captured by Private Isaac Rosenberg, in his poem 'In the Trenches', written when he was a soldier in the trenches during the autumn of 1916.

In the Trenches

*I snatched two poppies
From the parapet's* edge,
Two bright red poppies
That winked on the ledge.
Behind my ear
I stuck one through,
One blood red poppy
I gave to you.*

*The sandbags narrowed
And screwed out our jest.
And tore the poppy
You had on your breast…
Down – a shell – O! Christ.
I am choked… safe… dust blind – I
See trench floor poppies
Strewn. Smashed you lie.*

(*parapet – the built-up front part of the trench)

Trench raids

In the weeks leading up to the 'Big Push', British army commanders sent out orders for men to carry out trench raids.

Raiding parties

During trench raids, groups of British soldiers crossed No Man's Land at night to examine the enemy trenches, take note of their defences, including gun positions, and see how many German soldiers were defending each part of their front line. They were also instructed to either kill German soldiers or take prisoners who could be interrogated for information.

This raiding party was photographed the morning after a trench raid in 1916. Some of the men wear German helmets or caps, probably souvenirs taken from German soldiers they had encountered during the raid.

No Man's Land

Once they had crawled under the British wire defences, the raiding party made their way across No Man's Land as quietly as they could and crawled under the German wire, unless it had been cut beforehand. Private Walter Spencer later recalled: 'Well, you'd try and get down to a part of the enemy trench where you thought it was least manned, you see, and you'd grab a prisoner if you could. And of course he'd give a gawk and that's when the fun started…. it was a very hazardous job. We lost a lot of men on patrols, of course.'

Soldiers improvised to create weapons for use in trench raids, such as this club made from steel cable wound around a wooden handle studded with nails.

Casualties

Trench raids were unpopular among the ordinary soldiers as they often resulted in death or injury, usually for little gain. Lieutenant Ewart Alan Mackintosh led a trench raid near Arras, just north of the area of the Somme, on 16 May 1916. The raid was considered a success but Mackintosh was deeply affected by the death of three of his men. The experience inspired his poem 'In Memoriam' which he dedicated to Private David Sutherland and the others who died during the raid. The poem shows the strength of his love for his men, as well as his sense of responsibility. Mackintosh was himself wounded and gassed in August 1916 during the Battle of the Somme, and sent home to recover. He returned to France in October 1917 and was killed a month later, during the Battle of Cambrai.

In Memoriam

So you were David's father,
And he was your only son,
And the new-cut peats are rotting
And the work is left undone,
Because of an old man weeping,
Just an old man in pain,
For David, his son David,
That will not come again.

Oh, the letters he wrote you,
And I can see them still,
Not a word of the fighting,
But just the sheep on the hill
And how you should get the crops in
Ere the year get stormier,
And the Bosches have got his body,
And I was his officer.

You were only David's father,
But I had fifty sons
When we went up in the evening
Under the arch of the guns,
And we came back at twilight –
O God! I heard them call
To me for help and pity
That could not help at all.

Oh, never will I forget you,
My men that trusted me,
More my sons than your fathers',
For they could only see
The little helpless babies
And the young men in their pride.
They could not see you dying,
And hold you while you died.

Happy and young and gallant,
They saw their first-born go,
But not the strong limbs broken
And the beautiful men brought low,
The piteous writhing bodies,
They screamed 'Don't leave me, Sir',
For they were only your fathers
But I was your officer.

Bombardment

After months of planning, the British and French artillery opened fire on 24 June 1916, aiming their shells at the German front line north and south of the River Somme.

Labels on sketch:

H.E. SHELLS BURSTING IN TRENCHES

THE WHITE PUFFS ARE SHRAPNEL

CAPTIVE HUN OBSERVATION BALLOON

BÉCOURT WOOD

GUN POSITIONS IN DUGOUTS

FRICOURT VILLAGE LIES BEHIND THE FIRST TREE TOP RIDGE; MAMETZ ON THE FAR HILLSIDE.

FRONT LINE TRENCHES SHEWING WHITE

VILLAGE OF BÉCORDEL-BÉCOURT

This sketch was made a few yards from our battery position on the Albert-Bray roadside.

This sketch damaged through being sent to England in a friend's haversack.

Canadian gunner William Thurston Topham made this sketch of the bombardment on 24 June 1916 from his gun position. It shows that farmers' fields made up No Man's Land at this point.

A week of bombardment

As planned by General Sir Douglas Haig, the guns bombarded the German front line to wipe out resistance and allow stage two of the plan to roll into place – the attack. Bad weather meant that what was meant to be a five-day bombardment was stretched out over seven days. The noise was deafening and it went on hour upon hour, day after day. Over 1.6 million shells were fired and the intensity of the bombardment was unprecedented.

Royal Flying Corps pilot Cecil Lewis observed the bombardment from the air, where he was checking on the accuracy of the artillery fire, and later recalled: 'And so close were the shell bursts – and so continuous – that it wasn't just a puff here and a puff there, it was a continuous band. The whole of the ground beneath the darkening evening was just like a veil of sequins which were flashing and flashing and flashing and each one was a gun.'

The Germans

Deep below ground, the German front line troops were suffering terribly in their dugouts during the bombardment. Stefan Westmann, a German medical officer, lived through the bombardment, and remembered it as follows: 'For seven days and nights we were under incessant bombardment. Day and night. The shells, heavy and light ones, came upon us. Our dugouts crumbled. They fell upon us and we had to dig ourselves and our comrades out. Sometimes we found them suffocated, sometimes smashed to pulp. Soldiers in the bunkers became hysterical. They wanted to run out, and fights developed to keep them in the comparative safety of our deep bunkers. Even the rats became hysterical. They came into our flimsy shelters to seek refuge from this terrific fire. We had nothing to eat, nothing to drink, but constantly, shell after shell burst upon us.'

Misinformation

Meanwhile, back in the British and French front lines, the infantry had been assured by their commanders that the bombardment was flattening the German defences, killing all those inside, and that there wouldn't be a German to be seen for miles.

The German dugouts were typically 9 m deep and were well built, like this one captured on 3 July at Bernafay Wood near Montauban. Their design was so robust that most of them withstood the intensity of the bombardment, a situation that wasn't anticipated by the British commanders.

A 9.2-inch howitzer in action during the summer of 1916. The gun crew have laid out the artillery shells on the ground, ready to load them into the gun.

Over the top

Zero hour was 7.30 am on 1 July 1916. All along the British and French front line, officers had synchronised their watches.

Poised for action

On the eve of the battle, thousands of British infantry troops marched up to the trenches overnight, relieving the men who had been defending the line during the bombardment, which continued through the night of 30 June. In the trenches, men waited, many of them calming their nerves with their rum ration.

Mixed emotions

Many soldiers had written letters to loved ones that would only be sent in the event of their death. Surviving diary entries, letters and memoirs give us a mixed picture of how the men were feeling on

30 June 1916. Some were excited and confident that this battle could lead to the end of the war. Others were acutely aware that they were likely to die, and were filled with sad thoughts about never seeing loved ones again.

'Over the top'

Early in the morning of 1 July, soldiers moved into place. At 7.30 a.m. officers blew their whistles and men went 'over the top', scrambling out of the trenches or climbing trench ladders. Following orders, they started to walk across No Man's Land towards the German front line. In some battalions, such as the 8th East Surreys, an officer decided that footballs should be kicked ahead of his men, to encourage them to move forward.

Several mines exploded just before the launch of the attack, destroying some German defences and providing shelter in No Man's Land for British soldiers.

Almost immediately soldiers started to die, as a hail of German machine gun bullets flew across No Man's Land. In places, the German front line had suffered badly during the bombardment, especially where the French army were attacking, but elsewhere it soon became apparent that large numbers of German soldiers had survived.

Deadly mistakes

The recollections of German medical officer Stefan Westmann capture the moment the British attacked: 'They [the British] did not expect anybody on the other side to have survived the bombardment. But German machine gunners and infantrymen crawled out of their holes, with inflamed and sunken

This film still from *The Battle of the Somme* (see page 33) is often used to depict the moment the attack began on 1 July 1916.

eyes, their faces blackened by fire and their uniforms splashed with the blood of their wounded comrades… They started firing furiously, and the British had frightful losses.'

The British bombardment had not destroyed the German defences. In addition, the artillery barrage that was supposed to protect the advancing troops by providing a moving curtain of shells between them and any surviving German defenders had moved forward too fast, leaving time for the Germans to climb out of their deep dugouts and set up their machine guns.

The first day

Second Lieutenant Siegfried Sassoon, who was just behind the front line on 1 July, recorded these words in his journal at 10 am that day: *'I am looking at a sunlit picture of Hell....'*

Disaster

Wave after wave of men climbed out of the trenches to walk across No Man's Land, their bayonets fixed, but there was little chance that they would ever have the chance to engage in hand-to-hand fighting. Many of them fell back dead or wounded into their own front line trenches.

Death all around

As soon as the men of the 2nd Middlesex Battalion, attacking opposite the French village of Ovillers-la-Boisselle, left their trenches, they were killed or wounded by a hail of machine gun fire. A few dropped to the ground quickly enough to take cover, and found a shell crater where they could shelter.

This was the case for Lieutenant Alfred Bundy who wrote at the time: *At last the firing ceased and after tearing my clothes and flesh on the wire I reached the parapet and fell into our trench now full of dead and wounded. I found a few of my men but the majority were still out and most were dead.* Twenty-three officers and 517 men of the 2nd Middlesex Battalion were wounded or killed on 1 July.

When the whistle blew to signal the attack, soldiers left their trench, made their way through their own wire defences and walked across No Man's Land. Here, men of the 1st Battalion, Lancashire Fusiliers, with bayonets fixed on the end of their rifles, wait to go 'over the top' on 1 July 1916.

Wire

Those men that survived long enough to approach the German front line soon realised that the British bombardment had failed to destroy the German barbed wire defences. Corporal Arnold Dale later recalled: 'It was so thick, it looked solid black. I can't really say that I could pick out any single strand; it was so solid that in my opinion a rabbit couldn't have got through it.' Unable to move forward through the wire defences, the men became clear targets for German machine gunners.

Elegy for the dead

Although Lieutenant Wilfred Owen did not fight at the Battle of the Somme, his poem 'Anthem for Doomed Youth' talks of the tragedy of thousands of young men killed in action during the battles of the First World War. Owen was killed shortly before the war ended in November 1918.

Wounded men receive first aid treatment in a front line trench on 1 July 1916, the first day of the Battle of the Somme.

Anthem for Doomed Youth

What passing-bells for these who die as cattle?
Only the monstrous anger of the guns.
Only the stuttering rifles' rapid rattle
Can patter out their hasty orisons*.
No mockeries now for them; no prayers nor bells;
　Nor any voice of mourning save the choirs,—
The shrill, demented choirs of wailing shells;
　And bugles calling for them from sad shires*.

What candles may be held to speed them all?
　Not in the hands of boys, but in their eyes
Shall shine the holy glimmers of goodbyes.
　The pallor of girls' brows shall be their pall*;
Their flowers the tenderness of patient minds,
And each slow dusk a drawing-down of blinds.

(*orisons – prayers, shires – counties, pall – a cloth over a coffin)

Some men of the Tyneside Irish Brigade form a line of attack on the morning of 1 July.

The Pals

For many of the men who had joined up with friends or work colleagues to form Pals battalions, 1 July was their first experience of an attack. The Tyneside Irish, recruited from the Irish community living in Newcastle-upon-Tyne, suffered catastrophic losses. Made up of four Pals battalions, they attacked from reserve trenches where many of them were killed or wounded by German machine gun fire before they'd even left British territory.

1st Newfoundland Regiment

The 1st Newfoundland Regiment suffered one of the highest losses sustained by a single fighting unit on 1 July. The men had joined up when war was declared and left Newfoundland, then part of the British Empire, in October 1914. They were part of a second wave of troops who left their trenches at 9.15 am on 1 July. Out of 801 men, 710 were left dead, wounded or missing. The commander of the 29th British Division described their brave action that day in this way: *It was a magnificent display of trained and disciplined valour, and its assault only failed of success because dead men can advance no further.*

Small successes

In a few places along the line of attack, British troops were able to advance. The 36th Ulster Division, attacking left of the village of Thiepval, found that the wire had been cut and were able to push forward over a kilometre behind the German front line, past the Schwaben Redoubt, a notable German defensive position. However, at the end of the day, they were forced to retreat as they were running out of ammunition and they were isolated. None of the troops that had left the British front line trench on either side of them that morning had achieved the same success.

The French troops, attacking to the south, were able to take some ground that morning and move forward, occupying land around Hardecourt. British troops attacking immediately beside the French also managed to move forward to take the villages of Montauban and Mametz.

Confusion

As the day progressed, some senior commanders in their army headquarters set back from the front line found it hard to understand why they were receiving so little information from the officers who had led troops into the attack. They soon discovered why: 60 per cent of the officers were dead or wounded, leaving many troops without orders to follow.

As would become clear later, 19,240 British men had died on 1 July 1916, and over 38,000 were wounded or missing. These appalling losses were the worst ever suffered on a single day by the British army.

All along the front line trenches, commanding officers took a roll call after the attack, to see how many men had made it safely back to the trenches.

The wounded

Within hours of the battle beginning, the army's medical services were completely overwhelmed.

Regimental Aid Posts

Just a few metres behind the British front line Regimental Aid Posts, each manned by a doctor and several stretcher-bearers, patched the injured up as best they could. Some men arrived at the Regimental Aid Posts on stretchers, others were carried there by friends – and there was a vast number of walking wounded. Soon all the reserve and communication trenches were jammed with wounded men and stretcher-bearers.

The majority of the wounded had to wait until darkness had fallen to be rescued from No Man's Land by friends who had survived the attack. This rescue mission carried on all night, with the Germans doing the same on their side. Many wounded lay in shell holes for days before they were rescued – or died in the meantime from their injuries.

Artist Henry Tonks served with the Royal Army Medical Corps. In this painting, he captured the chaotic scenes at an Advanced Dressing Station (see page 27).

Evacuating the wounded

One of those injured on the morning of
1 July was Rifleman Maurice Baker (see page
12). A shell had exploded overhead, killing his
friends and sending shrapnel into his lower
leg. On his elbows, he pulled himself along the
ground to a Regimental Aid Post. From there,
stretcher-bearers carried him to an Advanced
Dressing Station, and eventually he reached
a Casualty Clearing Station. These basic
hospitals, often housed in tents, had operating
theatres and wards, but most men were sent
to a general hospital set well back from the
front line.

By 4 July, Maurice was able to write these
words to his mother from the VII Canadian
General Hospital, one of many temporary
hospitals at Étaples on the French coast:

Dear Mother,

*I am down in a base hospital with wounds
(Shrapnel) in leg & foot. I shan't be able to
walk for some time. I am being treated very
well & in spite of everything not doing so
bad. We had a hot time up the line. I was hit
very early on in the operations. Just as we
were about to go over the top. I'm in a most
awkward position for writing so I'll chuck it
up. You need not worry at all about me. I'm
going on all right.*

Maurice

Two days later he wrote again to say he had *a
little bad news for you. I have lost my right
leg. It is amputated below the knee….*

A nurse and a doctor tend a wounded patient at
a Casualty Clearing Station in France, 1916.

Back home

When men were well enough to travel,
hospital trains and barges transported them
to hospital ships, which brought them back to
the UK. Through July, London hospitals filled
to capacity with the wounded of the Somme.
On 31 July, Maurice wrote to his parents to
tell them that he was now in Bellahouston
Hospital in Glasgow, Scotland, as there was
no room for him in hospitals closer to home
in Suffolk.

Maurice recovered from his injuries, and
always considered himself one of the lucky
ones, but a vast number of the wounded died
over the following days, weeks, months or
even years. Shrapnel and machine gun bullets
inflicted horrifying wounds that were hard
to survive and, with no antibiotics, infections
failed to heal. Other men suffered from the
mental illness shell shock, brought on by
the horror of their experiences. Some never
recovered from it.

The battle continues

Despite the failure of the battle plan of 1 July and the resulting dreadful loss of life, that evening British army commanders met together and decided to launch further attacks in the days that followed.

False reports

Many of the battalions had lost so many men that they had to be formed into new fighting units, yet General Sir Douglas Haig wrote these words in a report on the evening of 1 July 1916: *Very successful attack this morning… All went like clockwork… The battle is going very well for us and already the Germans are surrendering freely. The enemy is so short of men that he is collecting them from all parts of the line. Our troops are in wonderful spirits and full of confidence.*

For most of the soldiers who had survived the attack on 1 July, this report could not have been further from their own experiences.

The Battle of Albert

1–13 July
The Battle of Albert is the official name for the first stage of the Battle of the Somme, which was actually made up of 12 battles over a four-and-a-half-month timeframe. After the huge attack on 1 July, much smaller groups of British troops focused their attention on the area south of Thiepval, where some land had been captured. Known as attritional fighting, the plan was to wear out the German defenders through constant small-scale attacks, much of it requiring hand-to-hand fighting. Painfully slowly, and with many more lives lost, the British troops captured Trones Wood, Mametz Wood and Contalmaison (see map on page 9 or 40).

A British sentry guards a German trench captured during the Battle of Albert, 1916. while his comrades rest.

Meeting the enemy

As the British troops advanced onto German-held territory, many of them saw German soldiers, known in soldiers' slang as 'the Boche', for the first time, both as prisoners of war and as corpses. Captain Robert Graves walked through Mametz Wood on 15 July, after it had been captured, and the experience inspired his poem, 'A Dead Boche' (below). A few days later, Robert Graves was so seriously injured that he was left for dead. However, he did recover and survived the war.

The cavalry, including the 20th Deccan Horse, Indian army, wait to attack on 14 July 1916.

A Dead Boche

To you who'd read my songs of War
And only hear of blood and fame,
I'll say (you've heard it said before)
"War's Hell!" and if you doubt the same,
Today I found in Mametz Wood
A certain cure for lust of blood:

Where, propped against a shattered trunk,
In a great mess of things unclean,
Sat a dead Boche; he scowled and stunk
With clothes and face a sodden green,
Big-bellied, spectacled, crop-haired,
Dribbling black blood from nose and beard.

Battle of Bazentin Ridge

14–17 July

An attack early on 14 July was much more successful than the 1 July attack. Preceded by a short, heavy bombardment of the German trenches on Bazentin Ridge, almost 22,000 troops attacked across No Man's Land. They caught the Germans by surprise and secured a section of trench 5.4 km long by mid-morning. The plan was for the cavalry to secure High Wood, emptied of Germans who had fled, but by the time the cavalry arrived, German defenders had crept back into the wood and were able to inflict great damage on the charging horsemen and horses.

ARE YOU A VICTIM TO
OPTIMISM?
YOU DON'T KNOW?
THEN ASK YOURSELF THE FOLLOWING QUESTIONS.

1.—DO YOU SUFFER FROM CHEERFULNESS?
2.—DO YOU WAKE UP IN A MORNING FEELING THAT ALL IS GOING WELL FOR THE ALLIES?
3.—DO YOU SOMETIMES THINK THAT THE WAR WILL END WITHIN THE NEXT TWELVE MONTHS?
4.—DO YOU BELIEVE GOOD NEWS IN PREFERENCE TO BAD?
5.—DO YOU CONSIDER OUR LEADERS ARE COMPETENT TO CONDUCT THE WAR TO A SUCCESSFUL ISSUE?

IF YOUR ANSWER IS "YES" TO ANYONE OF THESE QUESTIONS THEN YOU ARE IN THE CLUTCHES OF THAT DREAD DISEASE.

WE CAN CURE YOU.

TWO DAYS SPENT AT OUR ESTABLISHMENT WILL EFFECTUALLY ERADICATE ALL TRACES OF IT FROM YOUR SYSTEM.

On 31 July 1916, this pretend advert was printed in the trench newspaper *The Somme Times* in response to the terrible loss of life on the Somme. Humour was one of the ways that men coped with the death of close friends and the awful sight of battlefields strewn with bodies.

Battle of Delville Wood

15 July–3 September

Now that British forces were occupying Bazentin Ridge, they needed to clear Delville Wood of the Germans. The South African Brigade was given this task, which proved to be a very difficult one. From 15 to 20 July, hand-to-hand fighting and constant shelling from German artillery caused huge loss of life. Only 750 out of the 3,433 soldiers in the brigade remained, with the rest dead or wounded. Eventually the brigade was relieved by other troops, who continued to battle fierce German opposition over the next six weeks, before overcoming it in early September.

Battle of Pozières Ridge

23 July–3 September

An attempt to capture the high land around Thiepval and Pozières Ridge brought Australian soldiers into their first major battle on French soil from late July to early September. Early success was followed by fierce German counter-attacks as the Australian troops sought to secure the ridge and some of the land beyond it. More than 24,000 Australian troops were wounded, of which 6,741 lost their lives, but they did eventually achieve their objectives. Official war correspondent C E W Bean described the small village of Pozières as 'more densely sown with Australian sacrifice than any other place on earth.'

Australian troops load a trench mortar during the Battle of Pozières Ridge. Trench mortars were used to fire a canister bomb that damaged trenches – and those that were defending them.

Battle of Guillemont

3–6 September

In between the bigger attacks detailed above, the British army repeatedly launched small-scale attacks to gain territory. One of these focused on the shattered ruins of the village of Guillemont, which was almost completely destroyed by repeated British artillery bombardments.

Private Ernst Jünger of the German army described the scene in his book *Storm of Steel*: *The village of Guillemont seemed to have disappeared without trace; just a whitish stain on the cratered field indicated where one of the limestone houses had been pulverised. In front of us lay the station, crumpled like a child's toy; further to the rear the woods of Delville, ripped to splinters.* In early September, British troops eventually captured the ruins of the village from the brave German defenders.

Battle of Ginchy

9 September

Another shattered French village, Ginchy, became the focus of a British attack on 9 September. Again, the fierce German defence of the area led to great loss of life on both sides, but Ginchy was finally captured, largely through the efforts of Irish and Welsh soldiers.

By this stage in the year, villages and farms in the battle zone had been reduced to rubble and woodland areas to tree stumps, as portrayed below by Second Lieutenant J B Morrall in his painting of Mametz Wood in the autumn of 1916.

Mametz Wood: after the autumn advance, 1916. *The Abomination of Desolation* by Second Lieutenant J B Morrall.

Back at home

Reports of the Battle of the Somme soon started to filter through to families back in Britain and across the Empire.

The newspapers

On 1 July, London evening newspapers reported that the Big Push had started. In the days that followed, the general public read about the battle with great interest. Then came the impossibly long lists of the wounded and the dead in *The Times* newspaper – and local newspapers soon started to fill up with obituaries.

Local losses

Since many of the Pals battalions had been almost completely wiped out, some communities were particularly badly affected by the terrible loss of life. In the city of Sheffield, for instance, whole streets and factories were plunged into grief. Marjorie Llewellyn was a schoolgirl in Sheffield at the time and later recalled: 'And everybody rushed to buy the papers and [we] were horrified to find that so many of our city battalion were involved in this offensive. The news came through very slowly but there were sheets and sheets in the paper of dead and wounded...'

Hearing bad news

Just break the news to Mother
She knows how dear I love her
And tell her not to wait for me
For I'm not coming home.
Just say there is no other
Can take the place of Mother
Then kiss her dear sweet lips for me
And break the news to her.

(The chorus from a popular music hall song of the day)

In the following days and weeks, thousands of families received bad news. The War Office sent a telegram announcing the death of an officer and an official letter to the family of men below that rank. Other letters might arrive from the dead soldier's commanding officer or his friends – and then there was the farewell letter that many soldiers wrote before going into action. In parts of the British Empire, it could take weeks for the news to filter through.

NOTHING is to be written on this side except the date and signature of the sender. Sentences not required may be erased. If anything else is added the post card will be destroyed.

I am quite well.
I have been admitted into hospital
{ sick } and am going on well.
{ wounded } and hope to be discharged soon.
I am being sent down to the base.
I have received your { letter dated_____
{ telegram „ _____
{ parcel „ _____
Letter follows at first opportunity.
I have received no letter from you
{ lately.
{ for a long time.
Signature only.} G. Maurice Baker
Date_____
[Postage must be prepaid on any letter or post card addressed to the sender of this card.]
(C3509) Wt. W3497-293 2,250m. 4/5 J. J. K. & Co., Ltd.

Straight after a battle, soldiers used a Field Service Postcard as a quick way of letting loved ones know that they were alive. Rifleman Maurice Baker (see pages 12 and 27) sent this postcard on 2 July to let his parents know he was wounded.

The missing

Thousands of families had to live with uncertainty. Was their relative still alive? Had he been taken prisoner or was he lying injured in a hospital? Various organisations, including the Red Cross and the Graves Registration Commission (see page 45), supplied information about the dead, the wounded and prisoners of war. Some families placed adverts in newspapers asking for information about missing soldiers. After six months, the army officially registered men as 'missing, presumed dead'.

The Battle of the Somme

In the summer of 1916, over 20 million British people went to the cinema to watch the film *The Battle of the Somme* in the first six weeks after it opened. They could watch moving images of the preparations for the attack, guns firing and scenes immediately before and after the attack began. The scenes of men leaving the trenches on 1 July were filmed at a training camp, but almost all of the rest of the film recorded events as they happened. The film was even shown to troops serving on the Western Front. The British government hoped that the film would gain support for their war effort, especially from neutral countries, such as the USA.

In August 1916, Queen Mary was photographed visiting a street shrine in Palace Road, East London. Street shrines offered a place for people to stop and remember local men who were in the armed forces or who had already died in the fighting.

The September offensive

Back in France, General Sir Douglas Haig had been planning another major 'push' for weeks. In mid-September the attack was launched, this time with the help of a new secret weapon – the armoured tank.

Tanks

Work had begun in 1915 to design and develop an armoured vehicle that could carry men over shell holes and trenches, and crush barbed wire to create a pathway for attacking troops. By early 1916, a top-secret prototype tank was being tested in Norfolk. After the failure of 1 July, Haig and other British army leaders decided to bring the new invention over to France and use it in the attack planned for mid-September.

Battle of Flers-Courcellete

15–22 September

The British artillery bombarded the German front line in the area between the villages of Courcellete and Morval. At dawn on 15 September, as men left their trenches, their advance was hidden from the German defenders by early morning mist and smoke. The presence of tanks brought new confidence to the British troops. In the event, half of the 49 tanks broke down, but around the village of Flers they played a vital role in helping the troops, many of whom were from New Zealand, to capture the village.

Left: This map shows the territory that was won by the French and British armies by 14 July and 15 September 1916, during the Battle of the Somme.

Below: A tank photographed on 15 September 1916, the day tanks were first used in an attack.

GROUND GAINED
1 July–15 September 1916

BRITISH GAINS

FRENCH GAINS

Beaumont Hamel · River Ancre · Bapaume · Beaucourt · Le Sars · Hamel · SCHWABEN REDOUBT · Courcellete · Thie... · MOUQUET FARM · Martinpu... · Transloy · Pozières · HIGH WOOD · Lesboeufs · Morval · Bazen... WOOD · Sailly Saillisel · 14th July 1916 · Contentin le Grand... · Guchy · Saillisel · La Basselle · 15th September 1916 · Frégicourt · Albert · Fricourt · Montauban · Guillem... · Combles · MAMETZ WOOD · 1st July 1916 · Rancourt · Carnoy · Harb...court Maurepas · Ma...court · BRITISH 4th ARMY · Bouchavesnes · Curl... · Om...court · ...lancourt · Vermandoviller... · Suzanne · River Somme · Bray · Frise · ...illières · Péronne · FRENCH 6th ARMY · Herbecourt · Biaches · Flaucourt · Becquincourt · Maisonette · Dompierre · Barleux · Fay · Belloy-en-Santerre

0 1 2 3 4 miles
0 1 2 3 4 5 6km

Private Leonard Davies' recollections described his first experience of tank warfare: 'I was in a long, narrow trench, waiting to advance, when all of a sudden these tanks rose out of the ground behind us. They were terrifying-looking things, and they came over and went right over our heads. When the Germans saw them coming over, they didn't know what they were, they got scared. Superstitious race, the Germans. They turned tail and ran, and we chased them right back.'

Battles of Morval *25–28 September* and Thiepval Ridge *26–28 Sept*

The Battle of Flers-Courcellete had not achieved the longed-for breakthrough, but the British had advanced about 1.6 km over an almost 10-km length of front line. In late September smaller battles took place to capture land that they had tried to capture on 15 September, and of course on 1 July. The Germans fiercely defended their positions, leading to heavy fighting and more loss of life. However, the British army eventually succeeded in capturing a bit more territory, aided in part by the surviving tanks.

Prisoners of war

Whenever an army advanced, it inevitably led to the capture of prisoners of war. At this time, the British army was capturing a large number of German troops who had to be marched back from the front line under armed guard. Much manpower was required to guard and feed prisoners of war, but it was necessary work to ensure the fair treatment of British prisoners of war back in Germany.

German prisoners of war being marched to British-held territory during the summer of 1916. The German soldiers are wearing cloth caps.

Home leave

All home leave had been cancelled before the Big Push of 1 July. In late September 1916, the army started to allow some troops to travel home for a week of home leave.

'Take me back to dear old Blighty!'

Men longed for the chance of a few days at home, as expressed in the chorus of this popular wartime song written in 1916:

Take me back to dear old Blighty*!
Put me on the train for London town
Take me over there,
Drop me anywhere
Liverpool, Leeds or Birmingham,
Well I don't care!
I should love to see my best girl,
Cuddling up again we soon should be
Tiddley iddley ighty,
Hurry me home to Blighty,
Blighty is the place for me!

(* Blighty was soldiers' slang for Britain)

Home comforts

Arriving home, exhausted and filthy, a soldier's first job was usually to take a bath and get his uniform clean but home comforts could be hard to get used to, as recalled by Sergeant Charles Quinnell: 'The first night I came home, I got into my old bed and do you think I could sleep? No. Sleep wouldn't come. It was the first bed I'd laid in since I'd joined the army and when mother brought my cup of tea up in the morning she found me fast asleep on the floor. Now that's true. I'd got so used to sleeping hard that I couldn't sleep on a soft bed.'

Boots still covered with mud, soldiers arrive at Victoria Station, London, on their way home on leave.

Good times and sad times

Everyone made a fuss of men who were back from the front. Officers went to the theatre, while mothers and wives cooked favourite meals. Fathers spent time with their children. Men often felt that they must visit the relatives of soldier friends who had been killed. These sad occasions were made all the more difficult by the soldiers' efforts to protect relatives from the often horrifying details of how their son, brother or husband had died.

Time off in France

Soldiers also earned the right to time off in France in rest camps where they slept in tents or in barns and took the opportunity to visit local restaurants or cafés. They organised sporting contests, such as boxing competitions and football matches, and put on plays and other entertainments. As Rifleman Maurice Baker (see pages 12 and 27) wrote in a letter to his mother, … *once we are relieved and out of the trenches, we enjoy ourselves and we forget there are such things as trenches.*

The town of Amiens was a popular choice for soldiers with free time in the Somme area, but even the smallest village had *estaminets,* small cafés (shown here) where men could relax with a plate of omelette and chips, a beer or a cup of coffee.

Autumn 1916

As autumn weather settled over the Somme region, General Sir Douglas Haig was determined to continue the campaign. He still hoped that a major breakthrough could be achieved and was certain that the German defences were about to collapse.

The Battle of the Transloy Ridges *1–18 October*

This battle was formed of a series of attacks in the first half of October. Slowed down by atrocious weather and deep, sticky mud, the exhausted troops managed to capture the village of Eaucourt l'Abbaye but failed to make advances elsewhere. Fighting was fierce as they battled German counter-attacks. Thousands of lives were lost, with hardly any ground gained.

The Battle of the Ancre Heights *1 October–11 November*

In October and November, the British army launched attacks along the north side of the River Ancre, a river which flowed into the River Somme. They were attacking a German front line that had hardly changed since 1 July. Canadian troops played a large part in the efforts to capture the German defensive positions of the Schwaben Redoubt and Stuff Redoubt. Fierce fighting led to heavy loss of life but the troops did eventually succeed, and managed to occupy the longest trench on the German Front, Regina Trench.

MORE "FRAGMENTS FROM FRANCE"

The New Submarine Danger

"They'll be torpedoin' us if we stick 'ere much longer, Bill"

BY CAPT. BRUCE BAIRNSFATHER

[Captain Bairnsfather's sketches appear exclusively in "The Bystander" each week.—ED.]

Captain Bruce Bairnsfather's cartoons were printed in the *Bystander* magazine and sold as printed postcards that were popular with the troops. This cartoon sums up the conditions on the Somme in the autumn of 1916.

Battle of the Ancre

13–18 November

The final phase of the Battle of the Somme took place in ever worsening weather conditions as rain continued and temperatures dropped. Deep mud slowed progress to a snail's pace. After fierce fighting, British troops captured the fortified village of Beaumont-Hamel and the village of Beaucourt. Thousands more men died and thousands of German prisoners of war were taken. Finally, on 18 November, with the weather deteriorating, General Haig called off any further attacks and the Battle of the Somme came to an end.

Troops engaged in the Battle of the Ancre are photographed cooking up their rations and warming their hands in November 1916 (above).

Official war artist Paul Nash captured the devastated landscape caused by war on the Western Front in his painting *The Menin Road*.

What had been gained?

Historians continue to argue to this day about the significance of the Battle of the Somme and attitudes towards the battle have changed over the generations. Was it a total disaster that caused a horrifying loss of life? Could it be argued that the experience of fighting the battle helped the British army learn how to win the war?

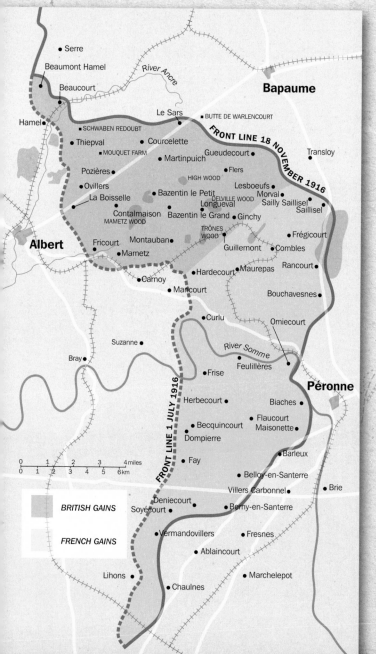

BRITISH GAINS

FRENCH GAINS

This map compares the position of the front line on 1 July 1916 and on 18 November 1916.

Was it worth it?

After four-and-a-half months of fighting, the British front line had advanced about 10 km along a 32-km stretch of the front line and both sides were still locked in the deadlock of trench warfare. The number of wounded and dead on all sides was horrifying: British forces – 419,654; French forces – 204,654; German forces – anything between 437,000 and 680,000.

In December 1916, General Sir Douglas Haig expressed his view that the results of the battle justified the losses. The British troops had helped to divert German attention away from attacking their French allies at Verdun (see page 8). In addition, the series of battles had, to a certain extent, worn down the German army. A German officer described the battle as 'the muddy grave of the German Field Army'; they lost so many experienced junior officers and other troops that this led to troop shortages in 1917 and 1918.

Artist CRW Nevinson was a pacifist who volunteered with the Red Cross when war broke out, but was sent home after he fell ill. He was an official war artist and this particular painting, *Paths of Glory*, was censored by Colonel A N Lee, the official censor of war paintings and artists in France, perhaps because he thought it was too sensitive a subject.

Although nothing can take away from the human cost of the battle, by testing out different tactics, such as the use of tanks (see pages 34–35) and the creeping barrage (see page 9 and 21), it could be argued that the British army slowly learnt how to use these tactics. In 1917 and 1918, these tactics helped them win the war.

Changing attitudes

In some sections of the British population, attitudes to the war changed after the Battle of the Somme. Some people lost confidence that the British and her allies could win the war, and began to wonder whether all the sacrifices were worthwhile.

Captain Siegfried Sassoon, who had fought on the Somme during July 1916, became increasingly horrified at the way older men in positions of responsibility encouraged young men to go out to fight. In 1917 he began to petition the government to make peace and end the war. His poem, 'They', was written on 31 October 1916.

'They'

The Bishop tells us: 'When the boys come back
They will not be the same; for they'll have fought
In a just cause: they lead the last attack
On Anti-Christ; their comrades' blood has brought
New right to breed an honourable race.
They have challenged Death and dared him face to face.

'We're none of us the same!' the boys reply.
'For George lost both his legs; and Bill's stone blind;
Poor Jim's shot through the lungs and like to die.
And Bert's gone syphilitic; you'll not find
A chap who's served that hasn't found some change.'
And the Bishop said: 'The ways of God are strange!'

What happened next?

For soldiers defending trenches along the Western Front, the winter of 1916 was a long, cold one.

German retreat

Between the end of February 1917 and mid-March, the German army voluntarily retreated to a new line of defence called the Hindenburg Line. This shorter front line meant that they could concentrate their efforts on future attacks. As the British troops moved forward, they found a devastated landscape and many deadly booby traps.

The USA enters the war

In February 1917, German U-boats had once again started attacking ships travelling between the USA and Britain. This helped to persuade the US government to declare war on Germany on 6 April 1917. It would take almost a year for all their troops and equipment to reach full strength in Europe.

Battles of 1917

During 1917 battles were fought out at sea, in parts of the Middle East and Africa, in Italy and on the Eastern Front (see page 43). On the Western Front, the British and French armies launched separate attacks: for the British, the Battle of Arras (9 April–16 May) saw some successes, but also fierce resistance resulting in much loss of life; and for the French, the

Australian troops, photographed on 29 October 1917, walking along a duckboard as they negotiated the muddy landscape of the Third Battle of Ypres.

Second Battle of the Aisne (16 April–9 May), was disastrous. During late April and May there were mutinies in the French army.

In Belgium, British troops fought the Third Battle of Ypres, also known as Passchendaele (31 July–10 November). After early success, the battle became one of attritional fighting carried out in appalling conditions for a total advance of about 8 km.

Russia leaves the war

Since the war began, sections of the German army had been fighting against the Russians on the Eastern Front. However, the Russian Revolution in 1917 led to the abdication of Tsar Nicholas II in March and to Russia leaving the war by signing a peace deal with Germany in December 1917.

Spring Offensive, 1918

On 21 March 1918, the German army launched an attack along a length of the front line that included the area of the River Somme. They captured thousands of soldiers, killed or wounded others and sent many into retreat. At first the Germans were able to advance 60 to 70 km but by May and June, the tables were turning once more as the British and French forces fought back, strengthened by US troops.

British and New Zealand soldiers follow a tank on 25 August 1918 during the Hundred Days Offensive.

Hundred Days Offensive

On 8 August 1918 the Allies pressed forward, gaining 12 km of territory. Now the Allied armed forces were bringing together all that they had learnt during the long war, as seen during the Second Battle of the Somme (21 August–3 September 1918), when they launched a coordinated attack using soldiers, artillery, tanks and planes. By the end of September, the whole of the Somme area had been captured and the Allied armies were pushing the Germans towards the French border. Elsewhere, the Allies were winning the war in the Middle East, Southern Africa, Bulgaria and Italy.

The Armistice

Before the Germans had actually been pushed back into Germany, they agreed to sign a ceasefire – the Armistice – on 11 November 1918. The fighting ceased after more than four years of war and ended permanently with the signing of the Treaty of Versailles in June 1919.

The dead of the Somme

Between 1 July and mid-November 1916, over one million servicemen – British, French and German – were injured or died in the area of the River Somme. By the time the war ended, over nine million soldiers worldwide had died – and more than 21 million had been wounded.

Battlefield burials

Soldiers tried as best they could to bury their dead comrades in hastily constructed battlefield cemeteries that dotted the landscape, sometimes using shell holes or sections of trench as burial places. It was grim work, especially as men sometimes knew the dead – they were their friends or even their brothers and cousins.

A huge number of the men who died during the Battle of the Somme lay where they had fallen in No Man's Land until the spring of 1917 as it simply wasn't possible to reclaim them until the area was finally in the hands of the British army. The British V Corps had the awful task of clearing the battlefield of bodies and creating new cemeteries.

After the Armistice

After the First World War ended on 11 November 1918, men working for Graves Concentration Units searched all the battlefields repeatedly for bodies and buried them in cemeteries that were often based around the original battlefield burials. For instance, Guillemont Road Cemetery was established around the graves of 121 men, most of them buried in 1916 after the Battle of Guillemont (see page 31). More than 2,000 corpses were re-buried here, the majority of which could not be identified.

This army chaplain (bottom right) was photographed tending the grave of a soldier buried during the opening phases of the Battle of the Somme in July 1916.

Guillemont Road Cemetery in France is one of more than 450 cemeteries and memorials that the Commonwealth War Graves Commission maintains in the Somme area.

The Thiepval Memorial to the Missing carries the names of more than 72,000 men with no known grave engraved on stone panels, most of whom died during the Battle of the Somme.

Cemeteries and memorials

During the 1920s and 1930s, people working for the Imperial War Graves Commission gradually replaced wooden crosses with stone headstones, laid out paths and planted trees to create cemeteries that were places of peace and beauty. Some of the families of the dead as well as ex-servicemen made pilgrimages to visit graves, memorials and battlefields. War memorials were unveiled all across the British Empire to remember the dead of a local community, school or workplace.

There are many memorials to men who fought in the Battle of the Somme, but none are more striking than the Thiepval Memorial to the Missing, unveiled in 1932. At its base are an equal number of French graves, marked by stone crosses, and British and Commonwealth graves, marked by stone headstones, commemorating the joint nature of the Battle of the Somme. On 1 July each year, a remembrance ceremony is held at the base of the memorial.

Remembrance ceremonies

On Armistice Day and/or Remembrance Sunday, at locations across the UK and its former empire, people gather to remember the dead of the First World War and all subsequent conflicts. The fourth verse of Laurence Binyon's poem 'For the Fallen' is often recited:

They shall grow not old, as we that are left grow old,

Age shall not weary them, nor the years condemn.

At the going down of the sun and in the morning

We will remember them.

Glossary

Active service Being on active service indicates that you are in a war zone, rather than in a training camp back at home.

Alliance A formal agreement or promise between governments.

Allies (also known as the Entente Powers or the Triple Entente) The countries which fought alongside Britain and France during the First World War. Britain, France, Russia (until 1917), Australia, Canada, Newfoundland, New Zealand, South Africa, India (including Pakistan, Bangladesh and Sri Lanka) and others fought Germany, Austria-Hungary and Turkey (the Central Powers) and Bulgaria.

Archduke Franz Ferdinand (1863–1914) Heir to the Austro-Hungarian Empire, Archduke Franz Ferdinand was assassinated by a 19-year-old Bosnian Serb called Gavrilo Princip on 28 June 1914. Princip was one of many Bosnians who wanted to free Bosnia from the control of Austria-Hungary.

Armed forces A country's army, navy and airforce.

Armistice The agreement signed by all sides fighting in the First World War to stop fighting at 11 o'clock on 11 November 1918 and start working out a peace treaty.

Artillery Field guns and trench mortars that fire explosive shells over long distances.

Attritional fighting A long period of conflict, aimed at reducing the strength of the enemy by wearing them down through many small-scale attacks.

Barrage An artillery bombardment concentrated on a particular area.

Battalion An army unit, commanded by a Lieutenant Colonel, made up of about 800–1,000 soldiers, divided between four companies.

Battle of Verdun A long, costly battle fought between 21 February and 20 December 1916 between the French and German armies and centred on the French town of Verdun.

Bayonet A long blade fixed to the end of a rifle, used in hand-to-hand fighting.

Billet Accommodation for troops.

Blighty Soldiers' slang for Britain.

Boche Soldiers' slang for a German soldier.

Brazier A metal stand for holding lighted coals to give out heat, or to heat up a pan.

British Empire Countries ruled from Britain, which in 1914 included India, as well as the self-governing nations within the British Commonwealth, such as Canada, Australia, New Zealand and South Africa.

British Expeditionary Force Britain's professional army, consisting of around 120,000 full-time soldiers in August 1914.

Captain An officer who commanded a company of between 120 and 200, divided between four platoons, each commanded by a Lieutenant or a Second Lieutenant.

Cavalry Soldiers on horseback.

Censor During the war, officials appointed by the British War Office to prevent unwanted information from reaching the enemy or the general public.

Central Powers Germany, Austria-Hungary, Bulgaria and the Ottoman Empire (Turkey) who fought against the Allies (see above).

Company An army unit comprised of four platoons, of about 50 men, each led by a Lieutenant or a Second Lieutenant.

Creeping barrage A curtain of falling artillery shells which fell in front of advancing troops to give them protection from enemy fire, and destroy enemy defences.

Division (of the army) Each of the five armies that formed the whole British army was divided into two or three divisions.

Drill exercise Repetitive fitness exercise used to improve the fitness of troops.

Dugout An underground room cut into the side of a trench.

Eastern Front The zone of fighting between Russian and German/Austro-Hungarian forces.

Enlisting Joining the armed forces.

Fourth Army One of five armies that made up the British army during the First World War. The Fourth Army was formed in early 1916 and many of its soldiers took part in the Battle of the Somme.

Front line The part of the trench system that was nearest the enemy.

General The commander of an army. Between 1914 and 1918, the British army expanded to have five armies.

Graves Registration Commission The part of the Imperial War Graves Commission responsible for registering the location, identity and other information related to each burial of a member of the armed forces.

Greatcoat Long wool coat which was part of a soldier's uniform.

Gun pit A depression in the ground, so that the gun could be hidden from enemy view.

Gunner Each field gun or howitzer was operated by a team of men, called gunners, each with their own role – loading the gun, cleaning it, aiming it.

Haig, General Sir Douglas (1861–1928) Army commander on the Western Front for most of the First World War, he was in charge of the plans for the Battle of the Somme.

Hindenburg Line Highly defended German trench system established in early 1917.

Imperial War Graves Commission (later Commonwealth War Graves Commission) The organisation established in May 1917 to care for the graves and memorials of the war dead.

Infantry Foot soldiers.

Mine A type of bomb placed just below the surface of the ground.

Munitions factory Private or government-owned factory that made shells, bombs and bullets, often staffed by working-class women.

Nash, John (1893–1977) An artist who fought in the war and became an official war artist in 1918.

Nash, Paul (1889–1946) Older brother of John Nash, he also fought in the war. He became an official war artist in 1917.

No Man's Land The area of ground between the two opposing lines of trenches.

Oath of allegiance A solemn promise. All new recruits had to take an oath of allegiance to serve the King and do their duty.

Obituary A printed notice of someone's death, often including biographical details.

Pacifist Someone who believes that war and violence have no justification.

Pals battalions Fighting units in the First World War formed of men who enlisted together – often they were from the same city, were friends, workmates or sportsmen.

Parapet The built-up front part of the trench, pointing towards No Man's Land.

Patriotism A strong feeling of support for one's country.

Pilgrimage A journey to a place of significance.

Platoon A division of the army, commanded by a Lieutenant or a Second Lieutenant, comprising about 50 men. Within each platoon were four sections of about 12 men.

Poison gas Chlorine, mustard gas, bromine or phosgene, used as a weapon of war against the enemy.

Rank A position in the hierarchy of the armed forces.

Ration A set amount of food given to each soldier daily.

Red Cross An international society originally formed in 1863 to train volunteers to provide help to relieve suffering during war.

Regiment An infantry regiment was the overall administrative unit of the army, made up of several battalions of about 1,000 men each.

Roll call Calling out a list of names after an attack, to work out who was present and who wasn't.

Route march A long, fast march carried out by soldiers as part of their training.

Royal Army Medical Corps The part of the British army that is responsible for the health of servicemen and women.

Royal Flying Corps The part of the British army which flew planes and which became the Royal Air Force in 1918.

Schwaben Redoubt A formidable German stronghold, made up of a series of trenches and dugouts, which proved extremely difficult to capture during the Battles of the Somme.

Timeline

Second Lieutenant The junior officer in charge of a platoon. Four platoons made up a company, commanded by a captain.

Sergeant Major A Sergeant Major helped the Second Lieutenant or Lieutenant in charge of a platoon.

Shell A metal projectile filled with explosives and balls of lead (which could also be filled with poison gas or smoke).

Shell shock The psychological trauma that some soldiers suffered, as a result of warfare. It took several forms including: complete nervous collapse, stomach cramps, facial tics, shaking, inability to control the body, nightmares and an inability to sleep or eat.

Shrapnel Small pieces of metal packed inside a shell (see above).

Sniper A skilled marksman in the army.

Stretcher-bearer Each regiment had men whose job it was to be stretcher-bearers, administering front line medical treatment and carrying the wounded back to Regimental Aid Posts. The Royal Army Medical Corps also had their own team of stretcher-bearers.

Syphilis A serious sexually transmitted disease

Tonks, Henry (1862–1937) A surgeon and an artist, Henry Tonks was in the Royal Army Medical Corps and was also an official war artist in 1918.

Treaty of London, 1839 This treaty, signed by all the major European powers, guaranteed Belgium's independence and neutrality.

Trench A deep ditch in the ground used to provide protection for soldiers. The front line or firing line was dug in a zig-zag pattern so that exploding artillery shells could only affect a short length of trench. Two parallel lines of trenches were dug behind the front line – the support trench and the reserve trench.

Trench mortar A type of gun that was light enough to carry into position. It fired a canister bomb to inflict damage on trench defences and enemy troops.

Trench raid A small-scale attack on the enemy by a small group of soldiers who crossed No Man's Land at night to gather information, take prisoners or destroy an enemy position.

War artist The government paid war artists, many of them soldiers, to paint what they saw.

War memorial Usually a stone or wooden object with the names of soldiers who fought, or who fought and died, in a war.

Western Front The zone of fighting stretching between the Belgian North Sea coast, through France to the Swiss border.

1914

28 June Archduke Franz Ferdinand is assassinated.

28 July Austria-Hungary declares war on Serbia.

1/3 August Germany declares war on Russia, France and neutral Belgium.

4 August Germany invades Belgium. Britain declares war on Germany.

6 August Austria-Hungary declares war on Russia. Serbia declares war on Germany.

7 August Lord Kitchener calls for volunteers to join the army.

11/12 August France and Britain declare war on Austria-Hungary.

17 August Russia invades East Prussia on the Eastern Front.

23/25 August Japan declares war on Germany and Austria-Hungary.

23–25 August Battle of Mons: BEF retreats from Mons.

26 August British and French forces conquer Togoland (a German protectorate).

5–12 September German advance on Paris is stopped.

September–November Trenches dug by both sides.

19 October–22 November First Battle of Ypres on the Western Front.

1 November Russia declares war on the Ottoman Empire.

3/5 November Germans defeat British and allies in German East Africa (now Tanzania).

5 November Britain and France declare war on the Ottoman Empire.

11–21 November British-Indian victory against the Ottomans at the Battle of Basra.

24/25 December Christmas Truce on the Western Front.

1915

19 January First air raid on Britain.

24 January Battle of Dogger Bank (naval battle).

4 February German U-boats start to attack shipping.

10–13 March Battle of Neuve Chapelle on the Western Front.

25 April–January 1916 British forces fight Ottoman forces at Gallipoli.

22 April–25 May Second Battle of Ypres – first use of poison gas.

23 May Italy declares war on Austria-Hungary.

23 June–10 November 1917 Battles of the Isonzo between Italian and Austro-Hungarian forces.

22–28 September Battle of Loos on the Western Front.

15/16 October Britain and France declare war on Bulgaria.

1916

January British and Ottomans engage in battles in Mesopotamia (now Iraq) throughout 1916.

January/March British Act of Parliament brings in conscription (being forced to join the armed forces), starting in March.

21 February Battle of Verdun – Germans attack French at Verdun.

24–29 April Easter Rising in Dublin.

31 May Battle of Jutland (naval battle).

4 June Russian forces attack German/Austro-Hungarian forces on the Eastern Front.

1 July–18 November Battle of the Somme.

18 December Battle of Verdun ends.

1917

January 1917 British still fighting the Ottomans in Mesopotamia through 1917.

1 February Germany resumes U-boat attacks.

23 February–5 April German forces retreat to the Hindenburg Line on the Western Front.

12 March Start of the Russian Revolution; Tsar Nicholas II abdicates on 15 March.

6 April The USA declares war on Germany.

9 April–16 May Battle of Arras on the Western Front.

May Imperial War Graves Commission is created.

16 April–9 May Second Battle of the Aisne – French defeated by Germans.

1–19 July Russian attack on Eastern Front is defeated by German forces.

31 July–10 November Third Battle of Ypres (Passchendaele) on the Western Front.

15–18 October Germans are victorious over British forces in German East Africa (now Tanzania).

20 November–7 December Battle of Cambrai on the Western Front.

December Peace agreed between Russia and Germany.

1918

19–21 February British forces capture Jericho from the Ottomans.

3 March Russia signs a peace treaty with Germany.

21 March/April/May German forces launch the Spring Offensive along the Western Front.

1 April The Royal Air Force is created.

15 July-6 August Second Battle of the Marne: French forces successfully counter-attack German forces.

8 August Hundred Days Offensive: Britain and her allies launch a series of attacks along the Western Front.

21 August–3 September Second Battle of the Somme.

19–25 September British and empire troops conquer Palestine.

11 November The Armistice is signed. Fighting ceases at 11 o'clock.

1919

28 June Treaty of Versailles is signed

Index

Further Information

www.bbc.co.uk/history/0/ww1/
The BBC has dedicated an area of its website to the First World War Centenary, with links to radio programmes, interviews, iWonder guides and more.

www.iwm.org.uk/history/first-world-war
Access the Imperial War Museum's articles about the First World War. The museum also has a digital archive of photos, paintings and interviews relating to the war, as well as fascinating podcasts.

www.nam.ac.uk/exhibitions/online-exhibitions/britains-greatest-battles/somme
The National Army Museum's online exhibition about the Battle of the Somme.